Sensitivity and Empathy of Women of Black Colour

12-Week Workbook and Other
Inspiring Stories of Black Women

Dolores Maaike

Contents:

Chapter One

Inspiring Stories of Kamala Harris and Amanda Gorman

The Inspiring Story of Kamala Harris

Kamala Harris, a former California senator, becomes the first woman and the first woman of color to serve as Vice President in History.

Harris, a former prosecutor and trailblazing California attorney general, has broken down barriers throughout her career. She ran for president in 2020 but was defeated, but her debate results attracted national attention. Her close relationship with Joe Biden's late son Beau was one of the reasons that attracted him to her as a running mate.

Here's what you need to know about Harris:

- Name: Kamala Devi Harris
- Party: Democrat
- Date of birth: 20th of October, 1964
- Hometown: Oakland, California

Douglas Emhoff's family includes his stepchildren Cole and Ella Emhoff, as well as the father Donald Harris and late mother Shyamala Gopalan.

Howard University (1981, political science and economics) and Hastings College of the Law, the University of California (1989, J.D.)

What she used to do: From 2016 to the present, she worked on the Homeland Security and Governmental Affairs Committee, the Select Committee on Intelligence, the Committee on the Judiciary, and the Committee on the Budget as a US senator representing California.

When Kamala Harris is sworn in as Vice President of the United States on January 20, she will be the country's first female, Black, and South Asian vice president. "While I may be the first woman in this office, I will not be the last," the former California senator told a crowd in Wilmington, Delaware during her victory speech in November. "Because every little girl watching tonight sees that this is a land of opportunity."

Harris's historic run with President Joe Biden started in January 2019 with her bid for the 2020 Democratic presidential nomination. Voters learned a lot about Harris' political beliefs and values from the various debates and media interviews that followed, but here are ten things you may not know about the vice president:

Her parents are Jamaican and Indian immigrants.
Dr. Shyamala Gopalan, an Indian American immigrant and breast cancer researcher, and Donald Harris, an emeritus professor of economics at Stanford, gave birth to Harris on October 20, 1964, at Kaiser Hospital in Oakland, California. In the fall of 1962, the pair met as graduate students at the University of California at Berkeley and married the following year.

Her name is a tribute to her Indian ancestors.
To help maintain her cultural identity, Dr. Gopalan gave her daughter the name Kamala, which means "lotus" in Sanskrit and is another name for the Hindu deity Lakshmi. Davi, the vice president's middle name, means "goddess" in Sanskrit, which is another reference to Hinduism. "A goddess-worshipping community creates powerful women.

She has a long history of becoming a social activist.
A favorite family story started with Harris engaging in protest chants from her stroller as her parents marched

for civil rights in Oakland and Berkeley, California, according to a 2004 Los Angeles Times profile. "What do you want, Kamala?" Gopalan asked innocently after one of the marches. "FEE-DOM!" she shouted.

Harris and her sister, Maya, later led a rally in front of their Montreal apartment building when they were 13 years old, in protest of a policy prohibiting children from playing on the lawn. The policy was subsequently changed by the owners.

She likes cooking.

In a May 2020 Glamour interview, Harris remembered, "As a kid, I remember hearing the pots and smelling the food, and sort of like someone in a trance, I would step into the kitchen to see all this amazing stuff happening." "My mother used to say to me, 'Kamala, you enjoy good food.' You should learn to cook.'"

That's just what she did, and now the politician is renowned for her culinary prowess, recipes, and fondness for Sunday dinners. In a campaign video in 2019, Harris and actress Mindy Kaling made masala dosa together, and she also showed fellow senator Mark Warner how to make a tuna melt in an online video.

On Thanksgiving 2020, she tweeted her recipe for "Kamala's Cornbread Dressing," saying, "During tough times I have always turned to cook." This year, I'd like to share with you one of my family's favorite Thanksgiving dishes. I hope that whatever success you achieve in life gives you as much warmth as it has given me — even when you are separated from those you love."

Harris paid tribute to her late mother Shyamala Gopalan, an Indian cancer researcher and civil rights activist, in a historic speech after her victory in November, saying she had prepared her for this big day in her political career.

Senator Kamala Harris, nicknamed the "female Obama," made history by being the first woman, first African-American, and first Indian-American to serve as Vice President of the United States.

Harris paid tribute to her late mother Shyamala Gopalan, an Indian cancer researcher and civil rights activist, in a historic speech after her victory in November, saying she had prepared her for this big day in her political career.

Harris, 56, has a long list of firsts to his credit. She has served as a county district attorney, including as the district attorney for San Francisco, where she was elected as the first woman, African-American, and Indian-origin person to hold the seat.

She is also the first woman, the first African-American woman, the first Indian-American, and the first Asian-American in her capacity as vice president.

Harris was the third woman to be chosen as the vice president on a major party ticket when Democratic presidential nominee Joe Biden chose her as his running mate in August last year, realizing the vital role Black voters could play in his determined bid to beat Donald Trump. The other two were then-Alaska Governor Sarah Palin in 2008 and New York Senator Geraldine Ferraro in 1984.

Harris had her presidential ambitions before becoming Biden's running mate, but she discarded them due to a lack of financial support to continue her campaign.

She is the first Indian-American to serve in the Senate and one of only three Asian Americans in the house.

She was nicknamed the "female Obama" during the Obama presidency. On the "Late Show With David Letterman" a decade ago, journalist Gwen Ifill referred to Harris as "the female Barack Obama."

Tony Pinto, a Willoughby small businessman, later described her as "a young, female version of the president."

She is loyal to Barack Obama, the first black president of the United States, who supported her in many elections, including the US Senate election in 2016.

Harris was born to a Black father and an Indian mother, both of whom were immigrants. Donald Harris, her father, was born in Jamaica, and Shyamala Gopalan, her mother, was born in Chennai and immigrated to the United States in 1958. She, on the other hand, clearly considers herself an 'American.'

Harris was raised mainly by her Hindu single mother after her parents divorced. Her mother, she claims, embraced the black culture and instilled it in her two daughters, Kamala and her younger sister Maya. Harris grew up proudly African American while accepting her Indian roots. She often accompanied her mother on trips to India.

Gopalan Balachandran, Harris' maternal uncle in Delhi, described her as a "fighter" who hoped that her high-ranking role would give Indians in the US "greater access" in dealing with the US administration.

In her autobiography The Truths We Hold, she wrote, "My mother knew very well that she was raising two black daughters." "She knew Maya and I would be seen as black girls in her adopted homeland, and she was determined to make sure we matured into confident, proud black women."

Harris grew up in Berkeley and was born in Oakland. Her mother was a professor at McGill University in Montreal, so she spent her high school years in French-speaking Canada.

According to the Biden-Harris joint campaign website, her mother told her as a child, "Don't sit around and whine about things, do something," which is what motivates Kamala every day.

"As the first Black and Indian-American woman to serve in the United States Senate, Kamala Harris grew up believing in America's promise and working to ensure that promise is realized for all Americans," the statement reads.

She went to Howard University in the United States for four years, which she has described as one of the most formative experiences of her life.

She went on to get her law degree from the University of California, Hastings and started working for the Alameda County District Attorney's Office after Howard.

In 2003, she was appointed as San Francisco's top prosecutor, and in 2010, she was elected as California's attorney general, becoming the first woman and the first black person to hold the position.

Harris developed a reputation as one of the Democratic Party's rising stars during her nearly two terms as attorney general. In 2017, she was elected as California's junior US senator.

"Kamala has devoted her life to the fight against injustice. Her mother, Shyamala, an Indian-American refugee, activist, and breast cancer researcher, "inspires her passion," according to her website.

For the past six years, Harris has been married to lawyer Douglas Emhoff. Ella and Cole, her two stepchildren, are an "endless source of affection and pure joy" for her.

Harris would "make history as the first woman, first Black woman, the first woman of South Asian origin, and first daughter of immigrants ever elected to national office in this country," according to Biden.

The position of Harris as Vice President will be more than symbolic. She is likely to exercise tremendous influence during Biden's presidency, unlike her predecessors.

And if Biden, who will be 82 when his first term ends in 2024, chooses not to seek re-election, Harris will be the strong favorite for the Democratic Party's nomination.

The Inspiring Story of Amanda Gorman

As she recited her poem "The Hill We Climb," the 22-year-old writer and first-ever National Youth Poet Laureate took the country's breath away and became an inspiration for the next generation.

All eyes were on a young, rising star named Amanda Gorman during the final moments of a stunning, historic Inauguration Day, where President Joe Biden and Vice President Kamala Harris (the first female, Black, and Asian vice president) were sworn into office. The 22-year-old from Los Angeles, California, became the youngest Inaugural Poet in US history when she read her poem "The Hill We Climb" at the ceremony.

Here's a short rundown of what we know about the talented author, who aspires to be President of the United States one day.

Gorman, who was born and raised in Los Angeles, fell in love with poetry after hearing her teacher read "Dandelion Wine" by Ray Bradbury to the class. To deal with her speech impediment, she turned to fiction. Gorman had trouble pronouncing those sounds, much as President Biden did when he was younger.

Gorman told the Los Angeles Times, "I don't look at my impairment as a weakness." "This has shaped me into the artist I am and the storyteller I aspire to be. If you have to teach yourself how to pronounce sounds and be extremely concerned with pronunciation, you develop a sense of sonics and the auditory experience."

Gorman started attending weekly creative writing workshops and collaborating one-on-one with writing mentors at the age of 14 when she joined WriteGirl, a nonprofit organization in Los Angeles that encourages creativity and self-expression to empower girls.

"WriteGirl has played a huge role in my life. I've been able to pursue my goals as a writer thanks to their encouragement "Gorman stated to NBC. "Michelle and Dinah, two of my former mentors, deserve special appreciation. We wouldn't have been able to get here without you!"

"I have no doubt Amanda's messages of optimism, peace, and equity will help us all heal and move forward," WriteGirl Executive Director Keren Taylor said.

Parents may get their children interested in WriteGirl in Los Angeles, Girls Write Now in New York City, or similar local groups in their neighborhood if they choose to follow in Gorman's footsteps.

Before the game, the 22-year-old will pay tribute to pandemic heroes. As President-elect Joe Biden was sworn in as the 46th president of the United States, Amanda Gorman stepped up to the podium as the president's inaugural poet, joining the likes of Robert Frost and Maya Angelou. She was the country's youngest poet in recorded history, presenting at a time unlike any of her predecessors'. Gorman, 22, was asked to compose a poem to embody everything Biden represents—a poem about unity. "I'm not going to in any way gloss about what we've seen over the past few weeks and, dare I say, the past few years," Gorman told The New York Times, amid four years under President Donald Trump, a period no one can characterize as unified. Her poem, "The Hill We

Ascend," gained widespread acclaim, resulting in major pre-orders for her three forthcoming books, as well as a modeling deal with IMG and a reading spot during the upcoming Super Bowl LV. Here's who Gorman is and why she was born for this moment as she finishes one daunting task—inspiring a fractured country during a deadly pandemic—and prepares for another—reading to an audience of nearly 1 billion football fans.

PANDEMIC HEROES WILL BE HONORED IN GORMAN'S NEW POEM.

Three Americans will be honored as honorary captains during the Super Bowl for their contributions during the pandemic. Tremaine Davis, a Los Angeles teacher, Suzie Dorner, a nurse manager in Florida, and James Martin, a Marine veteran in Pittsburgh who volunteers with the Wounded Warrior Project and helps local teens, are their names.

Gorman's latest poem will pay tribute to these three, but it's unclear how.

AT THE AGE OF 16, SHE WAS Appointed THE YOUTH POET LAUREATE OF LOS ANGELES.

Gorman was born and raised in Los Angeles, where she discovered her passion for poetry at a young age. According to the Los Angeles Times, a third-grade teacher caught her attention with Ray Bradbury's poem "Dandelion Wine," and set her on a course to spend nearly every waking moment journaling.

She was named the Youth Poet Laureate of Los Angeles in 2014, and her first poetry book, "The One for Whom Food Is Not Enough," was published in 2015. Her work on race, feminism and the fight for civil rights rapidly gained attention, and she was named the Youth Poet Laureate of Los Angeles in 2014. She was then elected the first National Youth Poet Laureate in the United States while studying sociology at Harvard University.

HER WORK WAS Noticed BY DR. JILL BIDEN.

Gorman's dissertation was discovered by the new First Lady just days before the inauguration. According to the New York Times, she was watching Gorman give a reading at the Library of Congress when she asked if he might read anything for the inauguration. She was told over a Zoom call that she'd been chosen to present and that she'd need to get on a plane to Washington, D.C., as soon as possible.

Gorman told the New York Times, "They didn't want to put up guardrails for me at all." "The inauguration's overarching theme is 'America Unified,' so hearing that was their vision made it clear for me to think, 'Great,' that's also what I wanted to write about in my poem, about America united, about a new chapter in our country."

UNTIL THE NIGHT OF THE CAPITOL Uprising, SHE Failed TO COMPLETE "THE HILL WE CLIMB."

She listened to music that put her "in a historic and epic mindset" while writing her poem, according to the Los Angeles Times, including the soundtracks from Netflix's The Crown and the soundtrack from Hamilton. Gorman, however, encountered a snag in the weeks leading up to Wednesday, January 20. The pressure to write something so moving that it would change the nation, like Abraham Lincoln's or Martin Luther King Jr.'s addresses, was immense. She wasn't able to finish "The Hill We Ascend" until she saw a pro-Trump crowd descend on the Capitol earlier this month.

"We've seen a force that would shatter our nation rather than share it / Would kill our country if it meant halting democracy / And this effort very nearly succeeded / But while democracy can be periodically postponed / It can never be permanently destroyed," she added after seeing Confederate flags storm through the seat of American government.

GORMAN HAS DISCLOSED THAT HE HAS A SPEECH IMPEDIMENT.

Gorman, like the 46th president, has managed to resolve a speech impediment. As she prepared for the inauguration, Gorman told the New York Times, "The writing process is its excruciating medium, but speaking in front of millions of people poses its sort of fear."

She told NPR that she struggled as a child to pronounce those letters of the alphabet, such as the letter R, and that she had to constantly "edit and self-police" her voice. She worried about which words to use in her poetry when she first began performing because she was afraid, she wouldn't be able to pronounce them correctly.

"I'd be in the bathroom for five minutes before trying to find out if I could say 'Earth,' if I could say 'girl,' if I could say 'poetry,'" she explained to NPR. "And, you know, doing the best I could with the poem."

She finds inspiration in the poets who have come before her, especially Maya Angelou, who was deaf as a child. "I believe there is a long tradition of orators who have suffered, a kind of forced voicelessness, you know, getting the stage at the inauguration," Gorman says. "As a result, it's very special to me."

SHE IS CONSIDERING RUNNING FOR PRESIDENT.

Gorman plans to run for president in 2036, the first political cycle in which she will be old enough to vote, according to the Los Angeles Times. Her plans were solidified after witnessing Vice President Kamala Harris's historic victory.

"It makes it more imaginable," she said of Harris's election to the New York Times. "When little girls can see it, they can become it. And they can be whatever they want, but the representation for even for me—in order for the dream to exist in the first place."

HER NEW BOOKS ARE COMING OUT THIS YEAR.

Gorman will publish two books with Penguin Random House in September 2021. The first is The Hill We Ascend and Other Poems, a poetry collection that contains her inauguration poem. Change Sings, a children's book advertised as a "lyrical picture book" about a young girl on a "musical trip" with her parents, is the second.

Other Inspiring Stories of Black Women

As the various indicators of poverty, education and work placement show, black women suffer from discrimination in a, particularly acute way. In recent years they have gained importance in the struggle for their rights as part of a gradual process of articulation and cooperation with other social movements.

During the COVID-19 pandemic, protests against racism and discrimination around the world have shown that we are far from achieving equality. Black women face a multitude of injustices and cross-cutting inequalities, but they are also leaders and pioneers in their countries and communities. If a better and fairer world is to be created, gender equality movements cannot afford to leave anyone behind.

Throughout history and up to the present day, black women around the world have made extraordinary contributions to our societies, sometimes without any recognition.

Here are seven incredible women of color who fight oppression and discrimination and lead the way to create a better future.

Tarana Burke

Tarana Burke founded the "Me Too" movement in 2006 and has been supporting survivors of sexual violence, especially young women of color, for decades. Inspired by the Tarana movement, the 2017 "#MeToo" mobilization drew attention like never before to violence and sexual abuse in the public and private sectors. She helped publicly expose the extent and impact of sexual violence and led a movement for change that exposed women's voices and experiences.

Vanessa Nakate

Vanessa Nakate started learning about climate change at the age of 21 and a year later she started leading the Fridays for Future movement in Uganda. She is also the founder of the "Rise Up" movement, dedicated to amplifying the voices of African activists. In early 2020, Vanessa was cut from a photograph of young activists at the World Economic Forum, reinforcing her determination to promote the voices and experiences of African women in proposals for action against climate change.

Jaha Dukureh

After surviving female genital mutilation (FGM) and being forced to marry at age 15, Jaha Dukureh started speaking out against these practices and became a leading voice in the movement. Dukureh, UN Women's Regional Ambassador for Africa, is now the Director-General and Founder of the NGO Safe Hands for Girls, which supports African women and girls who survived female genital mutilation, and addresses its permanent harmful consequences at the physical and psychological level. Together with women's organizations and civil society, she helped the Gambian government to ban female genital mutilation by mobilizing young people and campaigning in the country.

Emanuela Paul

Emanuela Paul is a Haitian feminist activist. As the coordinator of the Beyond Borders Rethinking Power program, she works to end violence against women and girls, including people with disabilities. As COVID-19 impacts her community, Paul is rapidly adapting to continue raising awareness and offering services to women in need.

Dow Unity

Unity Dow, the first judge of the Botswana High Court, has stood up for women's rights and human rights both nationally and internationally. In 1992, Dow challenged national law that prohibited Botswana women married to foreigners from granting citizenship to their daughters and sons, and she won. Dow is also known for her sentence as a High Court judge during the Kgalagadi court decision. Dow and another judge ruled that the San people, considered one of the oldest cultures on the planet, had the right to return to their ancestral lands after being transferred by the Botswana government. You currently hold the position of Minister of Foreign Affairs and International Cooperation of Botswana.

Valdecir Nascimento

Valdecir Nascimento (59) has been a leading defender of women's rights in Brazil for over 40 years. In 2015 she was one of the organizers of the monumental "Marcha de Mulheres Negras" (the historic march of black women), which mobilized more than 10,000 black women calling for an end to violence and racism and claiming equal rights. Kind. Nascimento is the executive coordinator of the ODARA - Instituto da Mulher Negra (Institute of Black Women), based in Salvador, Brazil, and coordinates the Rede de Mulheres Negras do Nordeste do Brasil (Network of Black Women of Northeast Brazil).

Sensitivity and Empathy of Women of Black Colour

The stereotype of the sensitivity and empathy of a black woman is a cultural ideal and a psychological coping mechanism. Black women must respond to the difficulties of life by showing strength and hiding the trauma. The sensitivity and empathy of a black woman have its route from historical and cultural circumstances which have since have effects on black women's lives. The idea of black women as sex objects wasn't good, the early marriages of young black girls were evil, the rape, the discrimination and cultural rulings against women all shaped the sensitivity of black women. Despite these sad experiences, black women are very empathic, they have deep feelings towards people and humanity. Even when black women are praised for caring for their siblings, helping around the house, and excelling academically, their emotional displays of vulnerability, anger and resilience of family members. To become the strong black woman, they were meant to be, black women would have had to develop thick skin and a sharp tongue. They should swallow the tears and have a great tolerance for pain.

Black women's sensitivity arises in several ways, such as when a friend forgets to reply to my text message or declines an invitation to go out. It may seem small, but it often feels like their world is over. But there are also more important experiences. Many women of color have learned to ignore racism and negative insults, but they take each case personally. And it's even worse when they see a black girl become a victim of domestic, police brutality or suicide. They feel devastated to the core. It seems to be happening to them, or it could have happened to their sister, their friend or their aunt.

As a woman of color, the repercussions of committing a slip, of letting their sensitivity manifest, are severe. At work, their face more severe discrimination. Vulnerability is rarely rewarded in the corporate world, but as a woman of color, expressing your emotions can make a difference in carrying out your work because women of color are far less likely to be promoted to managers and they face greater discrimination in the workplace.

Being a highly sensitive black woman in a world where black women cannot afford to be vulnerable simply creates another hurdle we need to overcome. But we're learning to value our sensitivity.

Contrary to popular belief, sensitivity is not a weakness. Indeed, it is a fortress. But unlike the stereotype of strong black women, our sensitivity makes us strong in a different way.

We are good at feeling the emotions of others, so empathy is easy enough for us. Our extreme sensitivity means that we feel extremely deeply and makes us eager to help those around us and make their faces smile. And that kind of empathy is a unifying force, uniting us, our family, our community and so much more.

We wish women of color were appreciated in society and that we could open businesses, start schools and lead entertainment companies more often. We wish we had walked the runways, where we were the main attraction, and that we could have been the desirable love interest in more films.

But the fact that women of color remain at the bottom of the totem pole, the fact that we still struggle to make a place for ourselves in this world, often makes us really cry. However, the fact that we care means there is a fire there. And we choose to fan it rather than turning it off by pretending to be something we're not. Healing is a force that makes us a whole person, rather than a superficial idea.

While being forced to feel pain so deeply is often a handicap, it keeps us hungry for a better life and reminds us that we must be consistent in our mission to improve the collective life of black women around the world. The very fact of trying so much is a reason for our business and it is the reason for our daily activism to improve the conditions of others.

While being overly sensitive can sometimes be a drawback, it's not a weakness. Our idealism leads us to see the world for what it could be, not just for what it is. We see the potential for a more diverse and inclusive world. A world where all women are treated fairly without being invalidated by their emotions and a place where men can be vulnerable and truly feel.

Black Women's sensitivity makes them good listeners. We enjoy sitting quietly in a quiet room, listening to a friend, or reading. We don't need more encouragement than that! Nowadays, stimulation is everywhere and listening is incredibly underestimated, but our ability to manage silence and really listen is an indispensable trait in defense.

In addition to listening, we process information to respond, not to react.

Our active listening skills and depth of processing make us less likely to react and more likely to respond. Our current culture is full of reactions, and this is part of what contributes to the impression that everyone is screaming all the time. However, they have found that highly sensitive people are more likely to respond. We need more time to process experiences and information, and in many cases, our brains literally won't allow us to continue until we do. As a result, when we listen to our needs and trust our brain's natural strengths, our depth of processing means we are more likely to get thoughtful and meaningful answers.

We have a sensitivity to subtlety which helps to evaluate solutions. Our high sensitivity is probably one of the main reasons I felt called to this job in the first place. As I became aware of more and more stories of suffering people, based largely on the ignorance and shame surrounding mental illness and families suffering from damaged psychiatric systems, my heart could not bear the thought of doing anything.

Our sensitive nature means that my heart is easily moved by the pain of others, but it also means that we are sensitive to subtlety. Therefore, you are less likely to get angry at hearing these stories and more likely to take the time to work out each of the proposed solutions. Our sensitivity and ability to think and process very deeply gives us a gift of the subtlety of thought when confronting solutions that need to be compassionate and effective.

Representation is something we should take very seriously. As someone who has felt completely alone and unrepresented for most of their childhood, we should take a conscious effort not to neglect others and leave them to the same fate.

Black women are empathic by nature and this can be an invitation to respond to larger missions in life. We should take to our duty very seriously to understand that our mission is much larger than our agenda. We should start to improve the lives of others. Therefore, we need to take more parts in political places and offices, as our sense of empathy can generate a kind of activism that has a real impact.

Our world has such a plethora and variety of problems that it doesn't take long to feel discouraged. But we strongly believe that highly sensitive people are desperately needed in this time of confusion, pain, division and (legitimate) indignation. Our gifts of sensitivity to both our own needs and those of others have the power to revolutionize our social and political discourse into one of compassion, selflessness and meaning.

Chapter Two: 12-Week Workbook

Week 1

Feeling Complete and Enough

Week's wisdom

The only viable standard for judging or accessing your life is the standard you create for yourself. You will always appear not good enough when you try to measure

up yourself with someone else's standard.

Affirmation

I will never allow my feelings or anyone else to make me feel inadequatebecause I know that I am complete and enough

Encouragement

How do you feel about yourself? When you look at yourself what do you see?

What do you think about yourself?

Do you think you're a wonderful person or you look down on yourself becauseyou don't seem to like and appreciate who you are?

Buddy listen, nobody can make you feel better about yourself than you makeyourself feel. And let me tell you this right here: there's nothing that is missing inyou: you're created complete, whole and amazing.

We sometimes feel bad about ourselves and think something is missing in usbecause we are comparing ourselves with others. Self-comparison is one of the commonest self-esteem killers out there. It makes you misjudge yourself by cre-ating a false impression in you that you're not all that great. Listen, pal, you are who you are and you cannot be like anyone else. You are dif-ferent and unique and under no circumstance should you rate or judge yourselfby the standard of another because every individual is uniquely different. Also,you should understand that you're the one that sets the standard of what beauty/ handsomeness or what you want to define is to you, so you can always tilt it in your favor.

How you feel about yourself is your own creation. If you think you're beautiful or handsome, smart, intelligent, likable, deserving of love, blessed, etc, you will feel that way and vice versa. You control what you think about yourself and how you feel about yourself.

If you keep telling yourself "I am beautiful/handsome," "I am complete and enou-gh," "I am a wonderful human being," etc before you will realize it you will start feeling that way about yourself and start acting it out.

We feel bad about ourselves most times because we misjudge ourselves and say negative things too often about ourselves. You're not awkward in any way. You're not dull. You're not a slob. You're not a jerk. You're not stupid. You're not ugly, etc. Stop misjudging your look. Stop misjudging your appearance. Stop criticizing yourself. Stop making yourself feel bad about yourself. You are the definer of yourself and it is what you think about yourself and says to yourself that counts - not what someone else thinks about you or says to you.

So, see yourself as complete and enough because that is what you are in reality. Nothing is missing in you. You're made whole and you have everything in you to make yourself whatever you desire to be in life. You're complete, you're enough and you're amazing just the way you are. So, you have to see the awesomeness in yourself and be proud of yourself.

Declare these words aloud to yourself

I refuse to negatively judge myself; I refuse to bring myself down; I will always see the best in myself, and I will always hold myself in high regard. I am complete, I am enough and I am made whole.

Goals of the Week

MON

TUE

WED

THU

FRI

SAT

SUN

REFLECTION ON ENCOURAGEMENT

....
....
....
....
....
....
....
....
....
....
....
....
....
....
....
....
....
....
....
....
....
....
....
....

Daily Journal

MON	TUE	WED	THU	FRI	SAT	SUN	DATE:
○	○	○	○	○	○	○	

SLEPT HOURS:

TODAY ENARGY LEVEL:

DONT FORGET:

EXERCISE:

TODAY HIGHLIGHTS

TODAY THOUGHTS

TODAY'S GRATITUDE

HOW TO MAKE TOMMOROW BETTER

NOTES

Daily Journal

MON TUE WED THU FRI SAT SUN   DATE:
○   ○   ○   ○   ○   ○   ○

SLEPT HOURS:

TODAY ENARGY LEVEL:

DONT FORGET:

EXERCISE:

TODAY HIGHLIGHTS

TODAY THOUGHTS

TODAY'S GRATITUDE

HOW TO MAKE TOMMOROW BETTER

NOTES

Daily Journal

MON   TUE   WED   THU   FRI   SAT   SUN

○   ○   ○   ○   ○   ○   ○   DATE:

SLEPT HOURS:

TODAY ENARGY LEVEL:

DONT FORGET:

EXERCISE:

TODAY HIGHLIGHTS

TODAY THOUGHTS

TODAY'S GRATITUDE

HOW TO MAKE TOMMOROW BETTER

NOTES

Daily Journal

MON   TUE   WED   THU   FRI   SAT   SUN   DATE:

○   ○   ○   ○   ○   ○   ○

SLEPT HOURS:

TODAY ENARGY LEVEL:

DONT FORGET:

EXERCISE:

TODAY HIGHLIGHTS

TODAY THOUGHTS

TODAY'S GRATITUDE

HOW TO MAKE TOMMOROW BETTER

NOTES

Daily Journal

MON   TUE   WED   THU   FRI   SAT   SUN   DATE:

○   ○   ○   ○   ○   ○   ○

SLEPT HOURS:

TODAY ENARGY LEVEL:

DONT FORGET:

EXERCISE:

TODAY HIGHLIGHTS

TODAY THOUGHTS

TODAY'S GRATITUDE

HOW TO MAKE TOMMOROW BETTER

NOTES

Daily Journal

MON   TUE   WED   THU   FRI   SAT   SUN   DATE:

○   ○   ○   ○   ○   ○   ○

SLEPT HOURS:

TODAY ENARGY LEVEL:

DONT FORGET:

EXERCISE:

TODAY HIGHLIGHTS

TODAY THOUGHTS

TODAY'S GRATITUDE

HOW TO MAKE TOMMOROW BETTER

NOTES

Daily Journal

MON	TUE	WED	THU	FRI	SAT	SUN	DATE:
○	○	○	○	○	○	○	

SLEPT HOURS:

TODAY ENARGY LEVEL:

DONT FORGET:

EXERCISE:

TODAY HIGHLIGHTS

TODAY THOUGHTS

TODAY'S GRATITUDE

HOW TO MAKE TOMMOROW BETTER

NOTES

Week2

Being Different Is a Good Thing

Week's wisdom

Self-limitation is trying to be like or copy someone else when you know both of you are completely different. Our world will be a very boring and uninteresting place if everyone else is like you or you're like everyone else. So always be yourself because that is the best person you can ever be – not someone else.

Affirmation

I embrace my uniqueness and I refuse to compare myself with anyone.

Encouragement

Being different is a good thing. Being yourself is one of the best things that you can do for yourself in life because that is the only way you can be at peace with yourself and function at your best. The best person that you can be in life is yourself. How you act and do things is unique to you, so don't ever be afraid of being who you are because of what the people around you may say or do. It's much better for you to be yourself and be called names than for you to live a fake life and get fake praises. Besides, you can only get genuine friends by being yourself, so be proud of yourself and make the people around you see you as you are.

Anyone that cannot like you or be with you for who you are doesn't really like you. And you can only be sure of people's love or likeness for you when you're portraying the real you.

Don't ever wish to be like someone else or try to copy anyone's behavior. Don't also compare yourself with anyone else because everyone is different and unique in their own way. No one can be like you, and you can't be like anyone else. So embrace yourself, be proud of yourself, and express yourself for all to see. You're different, you're unique and you should be proud of who you are. So don't ever be scared or ashamed to express your uniqueness because you limit yourself when you do that.

Declare these words aloud to yourself

I am different, I am unique and I accept my difference and uniqueness. I will be myself and I will let people see me for who I am because I am proud of who I am.

Goals of the Week

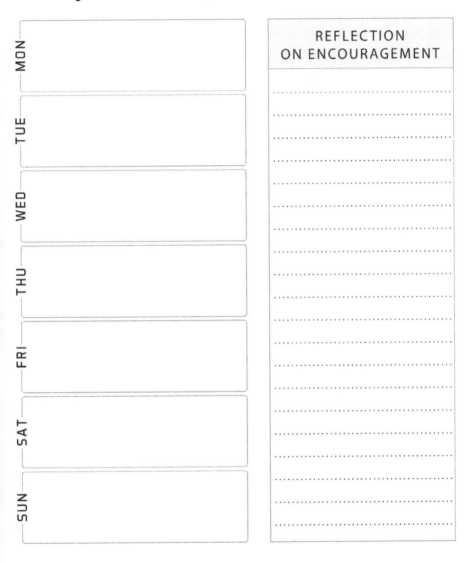

MON	
TUE	
WED	
THU	
FRI	
SAT	
SUN	

REFLECTION ON ENCOURAGEMENT

Daily Journal

MON TUE WED THU FRI SAT SUN
○   ○   ○   ○   ○   ○   ○   DATE:

SLEPT HOURS:

TODAY ENARGY LEVEL:

DONT FORGET:

EXERCISE:

TODAY HIGHLIGHTS

TODAY THOUGHTS

TODAY'S GRATITUDE

HOW TO MAKE TOMMOROW BETTER

NOTES

Daily Journal

MON   TUE   WED   THU   FRI   SAT   SUN

○   ○   ○   ○   ○   ○   ○   DATE:

SLEPT HOURS:

TODAY ENARGY LEVEL:

DONT FORGET:

EXERCISE:

TODAY HIGHLIGHTS

TODAY THOUGHTS

TODAY'S GRATITUDE

HOW TO MAKE TOMMOROW BETTER

NOTES

Daily Journal

MON ○   TUE ○   WED ○   THU ○   FRI ○   SAT ○   SUN ○   DATE:

SLEPT HOURS:

TODAY ENARGY LEVEL:

DONT FORGET:

EXERCISE:

TODAY HIGHLIGHTS

TODAY THOUGHTS

TODAY'S GRATITUDE

HOW TO MAKE TOMMOROW BETTER

NOTES

Daily Journal

MON	TUE	WED	THU	FRI	SAT	SUN	DATE:
○	○	○	○	○	○	○	

SLEPT HOURS:

TODAY ENARGY LEVEL:

DONT FORGET:

EXERCISE:

TODAY HIGHLIGHTS

TODAY THOUGHTS

TODAY'S GRATITUDE

HOW TO MAKE TOMMOROW BETTER

NOTES

Daily Journal

MON TUE WED THU FRI SAT SUN
○   ○   ○   ○   ○   ○   ○   DATE:

SLEPT HOURS:

TODAY ENARGY LEVEL:

DONT FORGET:

EXERCISE:

TODAY HIGHLIGHTS

TODAY THOUGHTS

TODAY'S GRATITUDE

HOW TO MAKE TOMMOROW BETTER

NOTES

Daily Journal

MON   TUE   WED   THU   FRI   SAT   SUN
○   ○   ○   ○   ○   ○   ○   DATE:

SLEPT HOURS:

TODAY ENARGY LEVEL:

DONT FORGET:

EXERCISE:

TODAY HIGHLIGHTS

TODAY THOUGHTS

TODAY'S GRATITUDE

HOW TO MAKE TOMMOROW BETTER

NOTES

Daily Journal

MON ○ TUE ○ WED ○ THU ○ FRI ○ SAT ○ SUN ○ DATE:

SLEPT HOURS:

TODAY ENARGY LEVEL:

DONT FORGET:

EXERCISE:

TODAY HIGHLIGHTS

TODAY THOUGHTS

TODAY'S GRATITUDE

HOW TO MAKE TOMMOROW BETTER

NOTES

Week3

You Have It in You

Week's wisdom

*One Of The Greatest Disservice A
Man Can Do To
Himself/Herself Is To Be Blind Or Unaware
Of His/Her Abilities. If You Don't Know You
Have It, You Can Never Utilize It.*

Affirmation

I have a lot of interesting stuffs inside of me

Encouragement

Do you know that you have lots of awesome abilities inside of you?

Sometimes, we are unaware of what we are made up of and capable of because we've not spent time looking deep down into ourselves. You have in you the abilities to create the type of life that you desire, but you have to search and discover such abilities from within you and nurture them.

Every human is blessed with awesome abilities, but until you discover such ability you can never make use of them.

So, start searching deep within yourself, observe yourself and start taking note of the things that you're good at. Some of what you may discover may seem inconsequential to you initially, but I must let you understand that no ability is a waste and with time you will begin to see its usefulness and value.

Don't neglect any special thing that you discover you can do seamlessly. Give it attention and develop it more. There's nothing in you that is useless. Everything has a purpose. Even if you may not be able to find a purpose for that special ability that you have discovered right now, don't neglect it because you will find its purpose with time.

You are a walking talent and you have so many abilities in you waiting for your discovery and manifestation. Don't look down on yourself. Don't rule yourself out on anything. You have the ability in you to get anything done.

It may take time some time, and sometimes it may require a little extra effort from you to develop such ability, and if you can be patient enough to do what it'll take to discover and develop the awesome stuff lying within you, you'll realize that there's nothing that you can't do or attempt because you already have the abilities in you to get them done.

Declare these words aloud to yourself

I am a blessed child; I am not empty; I have in me the abilities to make my life what I want it to be and I will never allow my abilities to be wasted or lie dormant.

Goals of the Week

MON

TUE

WED

THU

FRI

SAT

SUN

REFLECTION ON ENCOURAGEMENT

Daily Journal

MON TUE WED THU FRI SAT SUN
○   ○   ○   ○   ○   ○   ○   DATE:

SLEPT HOURS:

TODAY ENARGY LEVEL:

DONT FORGET:

EXERCISE:

TODAY HIGHLIGHTS

TODAY THOUGHTS

TODAY'S GRATITUDE

HOW TO MAKE TOMMOROW BETTER

NOTES

Daily Journal

MON   TUE   WED   THU   FRI   SAT   SUN
○   ○   ○   ○   ○   ○   ○   DATE:

SLEPT HOURS:

TODAY ENARGY LEVEL:

DONT FORGET:

EXERCISE:

TODAY HIGHLIGHTS

TODAY THOUGHTS

TODAY'S GRATITUDE

HOW TO MAKE TOMMOROW BETTER

NOTES

Daily Journal

MON	TUE	WED	THU	FRI	SAT	SUN	DATE:
◯	◯	◯	◯	◯	◯	◯	

SLEPT HOURS:

TODAY ENARGY LEVEL:

DONT FORGET:

EXERCISE:

TODAY HIGHLIGHTS

TODAY THOUGHTS

TODAY'S GRATITUDE

HOW TO MAKE TOMMOROW BETTER

NOTES

Daily Journal

MON ⃝ TUE ⃝ WED ⃝ THU ⃝ FRI ⃝ SAT ⃝ SUN ⃝ DATE:

SLEPT HOURS:

TODAY ENARGY LEVEL:

DONT FORGET:

EXERCISE:

TODAY HIGHLIGHTS

TODAY THOUGHTS

TODAY'S GRATITUDE

HOW TO MAKE TOMMOROW BETTER

NOTES

Daily Journal

MON ○   TUE ○   WED ○   THU ○   FRI ○   SAT ○   SUN ○   DATE:

SLEPT HOURS:

TODAY ENARGY LEVEL:

DONT FORGET:

EXERCISE:

TODAY HIGHLIGHTS

TODAY THOUGHTS

TODAY'S GRATITUDE

HOW TO MAKE TOMMOROW BETTER

NOTES

Daily Journal

MON   TUE   WED   THU   FRI   SAT   SUN
○   ○   ○   ○   ○   ○   ○   DATE:

SLEPT HOURS:

TODAY ENARGY LEVEL:

DONT FORGET:

EXERCISE:

TODAY HIGHLIGHTS

TODAY THOUGHTS

TODAY'S GRATITUDE

HOW TO MAKE TOMMOROW BETTER

NOTES

Daily Journal

MON   TUE   WED   THU   FRI   SAT   SUN | DATE:
○   ○   ○   ○   ○   ○   ○

SLEPT HOURS:

TODAY ENARGY LEVEL:

DONT FORGET:

EXERCISE:

TODAY HIGHLIGHTS

TODAY THOUGHTS

TODAY'S GRATITUDE

HOW TO MAKE TOMMOROW BETTER

NOTES

Week4

Don t reflect it

Week's wisdom

If It Is Not Your Name, Don't Answer
to It or   React to It.

Affirmation

I am not the stereotype, I define who I am.

Encouragement

The stereotype is other people's opinion about a group of persons, ethnicity or race. This opinion is mostly based on observations of a very minute fraction of such people and such observation is used to describe the whole. The sad thing about stereotyping people is that the intention of the observer determines what he/she is going to concentrate on. And most times, the observer's intention is usually evil and so also will be their opinions.

When people stereotype, they hardly concentrate on the good traits of the people they're stereotyping because stereotyping is a tool of control. During the slave trade and the era of intense oppression of blacks, stereotypes were used to justify oppression, wickedness and evil done against blacks. So stereotyping people is a means of subjecting such people to a general disdain and make it difficult for such people to break free from their oppressors.

You remember that saying that goes thus, "if you want to hang a dog, first give it a bad name?" This is exactly what stereotyping aims to achieve. They look for a negative phrase and attach it to a group of people because they want to justify their evil oppression or treatment of such a group of people. This is why you and I have to reject every negative stereotype that has been placed on our kind.

They call us names and gave us many negative tags because they want to justify their evil treatment of us. If you're a black woman and you try to have an opinion or speak up for yourself they'll say you're proud, angry, loud and what have you. If you're a black man and your express your dominating personality anywhere they will feel threatened and say you're a thug, violent, drug pushers, etc. They are so scared of us and their modern way of trying to subjugate us is to place tags on us in the name of stereotype so that they can keep justifying their evil against us. Have you noticed that whenever a cop unjustly gun down any young black man they immediately put the tag of a "thug" on him and dig into his history to find a misdemeanor from his past that they can use to justify their evil act - even if his past has no connection with the event that led to his unlawful shooting? And have you also noticed that the moment they do that everyone will start elaborating the officer from his crime and start putting the blame on the one that was unjustly shot at? All these are the effects of stereotyping people. It's a tool for justifying oppression and we must all stand up to resist these evil tags placed on us by refusing to reflect them. Our men are not thugs, robbers, crack-heads and what have you. And our women are not angry, whores, welfare mothers, etc.

We have to start defining ourselves by ourselves and stop giving them a justification to continue their oppression of us. We have to watch our actions and how we live our lives. We have to start reflecting on who we really are for the world to see and make them understand that they are wrong for placing those evil tags on us. We are not the stereotypes, so we shouldn't allow anyone to psychologically control our behaviors and actions with their evil stereotypes. Don't give anyone such power over you. Don't give anyone the justification to oppress you or treat you unjustly. If you don't reflect or act the stereotypes they will have nothing on you and can hardly deny you what you truly deserve. What anyone calls you is inconsequential if you don't act it. Some of our brothers and sisters are still playing their scripts by falling for their negative stereotypes. We have to be wise and start carving a new name for ourselves. You're not a junkie, you're not a pimp, you're not a thug, you're not violent and you're not any negative stereotype out there that is being used to control us and put us at their mercy. That is not who you are. Stop getting emotional whenever anyone tries to get at you by tagging you what you're not. You're not the stereotypes so don't act like it. Show them you're different through your lifestyle. Make them understand that so many of us are not what they are portraying us to be and we deserve to be treated right and respected. Our culture is not one of baggy jeans, sagging pants, violence, inordinate sex and irresponsibility. Our culture is rich and we have to let them understand that it is not what they are portraying it to be. If anyone is going to change our narrative, it is you and Wherever we find ourselves, let's give ourselves a good representation and disappoint anyone that's expecting us to conform to their negative narrative of us.

We are not the stereotypes, so let's stop acting like it and not give them a justification to keep carrying out their evil agenda against us.

Declare these words aloud to yourself

I am not what you say I am, I am not who you say I am, I am not the stereotypes and I refuse to conform to what you want me to be and keep giving you a reason to oppress me. I am not the stereotype and I will neverreflect what I am not.

Goals of the Week

MON

TUE

WED

THU

FRI

SAT

SUN

REFLECTION
ON ENCOURAGEMENT

Daily Journal

MON TUE WED THU FRI SAT SUN

○ ○ ○ ○ ○ ○ ○ | DATE:

SLEPT HOURS:

TODAY ENARGY LEVEL:

DONT FORGET:

EXERCISE:

TODAY HIGHLIGHTS

TODAY THOUGHTS

TODAY'S GRATITUDE

HOW TO MAKE TOMMOROW BETTER

NOTES

Daily Journal

MON TUE WED THU FRI SAT SUN DATE:

○   ○   ○   ○   ○   ○   ○

SLEPT HOURS:

TODAY ENARGY LEVEL:

DONT FORGET:

EXERCISE:

TODAY HIGHLIGHTS

TODAY THOUGHTS

TODAY'S GRATITUDE

HOW TO MAKE TOMMOROW BETTER

NOTES

Daily Journal

MON　　TUE　　WED　　THU　　FRI　　SAT　　SUN
○　　　○　　　○　　　○　　　○　　　○　　　○　　　DATE:

SLEPT HOURS:

TODAY ENARGY LEVEL:

DONT FORGET:

EXERCISE:

TODAY HIGHLIGHTS

TODAY THOUGHTS

TODAY'S GRATITUDE

HOW TO MAKE TOMMOROW BETTER

NOTES

Daily Journal

MON	TUE	WED	THU	FRI	SAT	SUN	DATE:
○	○	○	○	○	○	○	

SLEPT HOURS:

TODAY ENARGY LEVEL:

DONT FORGET:

EXERCISE:

TODAY HIGHLIGHTS

TODAY THOUGHTS

TODAY'S GRATITUDE

HOW TO MAKE TOMMOROW BETTER

NOTES

Daily Journal

MON ○   TUE ○   WED ○   THU ○   FRI ○   SAT ○   SUN ○   DATE:

SLEPT HOURS:

TODAY ENARGY LEVEL:

DONT FORGET:

EXERCISE:

TODAY HIGHLIGHTS

TODAY THOUGHTS

TODAY'S GRATITUDE

HOW TO MAKE TOMMOROW BETTER

NOTES

Daily Journal

MON ○ TUE ○ WED ○ THU ○ FRI ○ SAT ○ SUN ○ DATE:

SLEPT HOURS:

TODAY ENARGY LEVEL:

DONT FORGET:

EXERCISE:

TODAY HIGHLIGHTS

TODAY THOUGHTS

TODAY'S GRATITUDE

HOW TO MAKE TOMMOROW BETTER

NOTES

Daily Journal

MON ○ TUE ○ WED ○ THU ○ FRI ○ SAT ○ SUN ○ | DATE:

SLEPT HOURS:

TODAY ENARGY LEVEL:

DONT FORGET:

EXERCISE:

TODAY HIGHLIGHTS

TODAY THOUGHTS

TODAY'S GRATITUDE

HOW TO MAKE TOMMOROW BETTER

NOTES

Week5

What Are You Projecting

Week's Wisdom

You Give People The Power To Take Advantage Of You When You Make Your Life About Your Disabilities Or Weaknesses. If You Think That Something Is Wrong With You, You'll Always Go About Showing The World That Something Is Wrong With You And The World Will Certainly Treat You Like Someone That Something Is Wrong With.

Affirmation

I know I have strengths and weakness, but I choose to
concentrate on mystrengths and project them

Encouragement

Do you know that every human on the face of the
earth has things that they are good at or positive
attributes and things that they are not so good at?
But have you ever wondered why so many people
choose to concentrate more on their bad sides
(the things that they are not so good at or their
limitations) than on their good sides (their positive
attributes or their strengths)?
This occurs because a majority of such people are
still struggling with accepting themselves just as
they are. When you don't accept yourself just as
you are when you think there are more things that
are wrong with you than there are good qualities
in you when you're not pleased with who you are,
you'll get blind to your abilities or strengths and
you will concentrate more on your disabilities and
allow them to rule your life and weigh you down.

Every human you see on the face of this earth has both strengths and weaknesses, but it is the aspect of ourselves that each one of us chooses to concentrate on that determines how we're going to feel about ourselves, how confident we'll be in ourselves and how quality our lives will be.

If you see a person that is very confident, it is not because such a person doesn't have weaknesses, it's because such a person chooses to concentrate on his/her strengths and project such strengths rather than concentrating on his/her weaknesses and allowing such weaknesses to rule his/her life and weigh him/her down.

You can't know most confident people's weaknesses or the things they are scared of unless you're very close to them because they have learned how to not allow their disabilities to stop them from living and enjoying their lives.

It is not what you don't have or lack that is important, but what you do with what you have. Some of us are concentrating on what we don't have and struggling very hard to have them while we ignore what we have. We forget that it is by utilizing what we have that we can be able to attract or get what we don't have. Our strengths are the only tools through which we can correct our weaknesses or limit the effects of our weaknesses on us. But when you ignore your strength because you're not pleased with your weaknesses, you're giving your weaknesses the power to take over you and control your life.

Your outcome in life and how other people will relate with you are very much dependent on the aspect of yourself that you choose to give expression to and project. Are you selling/projecting your strengths or you're unconsciously betraying yourself before everyone by projecting your weaknesses for everyone to see? You have to understand that projecting your weaknesses for all to see will put you in a disadvantaged position because it will expose you to exploitation and attack. So you had better hide it from the view of others.

If people are always treating you in ways you don't like, then you have to look deep down within yourself and find out what it is that you're projecting about yourself to them.

Your strengths are yours and your weaknesses are also yours, but they act against each other. Projecting your strengths kills your weaknesses and projecting your weaknesses makes you blind to your strength. But if you want to have a vibrant, happy and interesting life, then nothing should stop you from discovering your strengths and projecting them. Find what you are good at, harness them and make a resolve to live your life projecting this aspect of yourself. The more you do this, the more your confidence will soar and the more interesting and fulfilling your life will get. You decide the side of you that people will see, which side of you are you reflecting on them?

Declare These Words Aloud to Yourself

I know I have weaknesses and strengths, and which of them I choose to concentrate on determines how I will feel about myself and how confident and productive my life will be; so I choose to discover my strengths, appreciate them, celebrate them and project them. I refuse to allow my little disabilities to hold my life to ransom and stop me from living a happy life. I will concentrate on my strengths and project them.

Goals of the Week

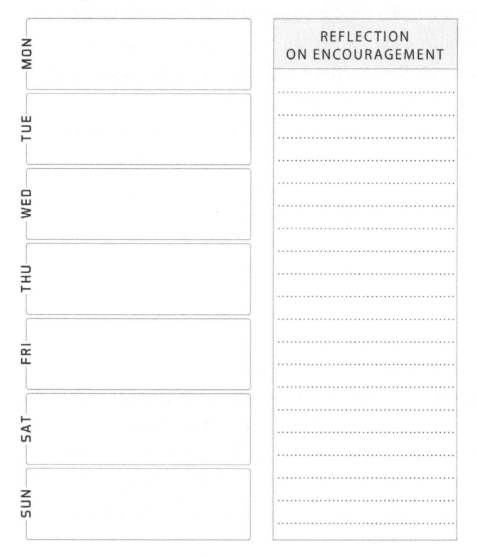

MON	**REFLECTION ON ENCOURAGEMENT**
TUE	
WED	
THU	
FRI	
SAT	
SUN	

Daily Journal

MON   TUE   WED   THU   FRI   SAT   SUN   DATE:
○   ○   ○   ○   ○   ○   ○

SLEPT HOURS:

TODAY ENARGY LEVEL:

DONT FORGET:

EXERCISE:

TODAY HIGHLIGHTS

TODAY THOUGHTS

TODAY'S GRATITUDE

HOW TO MAKE TOMMOROW BETTER

NOTES

Daily Journal

MON　TUE　WED　THU　FRI　SAT　SUN
○　　○　　○　　○　　○　　○　　○　　　DATE:

SLEPT HOURS:

TODAY HIGHLIGHTS

TODAY ENARGY LEVEL:

DONT FORGET:

EXERCISE:

TODAY THOUGHTS

TODAY'S GRATITUDE

HOW TO MAKE TOMMOROW BETTER

NOTES

Daily Journal

MON ○ TUE ○ WED ○ THU ○ FRI ○ SAT ○ SUN ○ | DATE:

SLEPT HOURS:

TODAY ENARGY LEVEL:

DONT FORGET:

EXERCISE:

TODAY HIGHLIGHTS

TODAY THOUGHTS

TODAY'S GRATITUDE

HOW TO MAKE TOMMOROW BETTER

NOTES

Daily Journal

MON   TUE   WED   THU   FRI   SAT   SUN

○   ○   ○   ○   ○   ○   ○   DATE:

SLEPT HOURS:

TODAY ENARGY LEVEL:

DONT FORGET:

EXERCISE:

TODAY HIGHLIGHTS

TODAY THOUGHTS

TODAY'S GRATITUDE

HOW TO MAKE TOMMOROW BETTER

NOTES

Daily Journal

MON   TUE   WED   THU   FRI   SAT   SUN

○   ○   ○   ○   ○   ○   ○   DATE:

SLEPT HOURS:

TODAY ENARGY LEVEL:

DONT FORGET:

EXERCISE:

TODAY HIGHLIGHTS

TODAY THOUGHTS

TODAY'S GRATITUDE

HOW TO MAKE TOMMOROW BETTER

NOTES

Daily Journal

MON TUE WED THU FRI SAT SUN
○   ○   ○   ○   ○   ○   ○   DATE:

SLEPT HOURS:

TODAY ENARGY LEVEL:

DONT FORGET:

EXERCISE:

TODAY HIGHLIGHTS

TODAY THOUGHTS

TODAY'S GRATITUDE

HOW TO MAKE TOMMOROW BETTER

NOTES

Daily Journal

MON ○ TUE ○ WED ○ THU ○ FRI ○ SAT ○ SUN ○ DATE:

SLEPT HOURS:

TODAY ENARGY LEVEL:

DONT FORGET:

EXERCISE:

TODAY HIGHLIGHTS

TODAY THOUGHTS

TODAY'S GRATITUDE

HOW TO MAKE TOMMOROW BETTER

NOTES

Week 6

What Are You Going to Do About It?

Week's Wisdom

Nobody is perfect, but everybody can improve. What are you doing to make yourself better?

Affirmation

I can improve on myself; I can be better than this, and I choose to dedicate my life to my constant improvement

Encouragement

You can improve: you can be better at that thing; you can make yourself look good; you can learn or know more about that thing that seems difficult to you by devoting more time to studying about it or practicing it; you can manage your emotion, you can become the best at what you do, etc. All you have to do is to find out what you need to do to make such improve- ent or development possible and follow it through. Self-improvement is the means through which we silent our imperfections and makes them less visible in us. But before you can start this process of self-improvement successfully, you first have to be at peace with yourself by accepting yourself just as you are because only then can you be able to see the aspects of your life that can be improved on and be able to figure out what you can do in order to make such improvement possible. Self-acceptance is necessary for self-improvement because it will enable you to go through such a process with a clear and unbiased mind and help you follow it through to the end. You may not be able to change who you are or who you're created to be, but you can improve on who you are. Improvement is all about making something better than what it was in its actual state.

But this requires desire, patience, effort, and determination. A short person may not be able to make himself or herself taller, but a short person can be able to make himself/herself more attractive by choosing to look good and outstanding by performing excellently in his/her endeavor. The shortest person in a crowd can make himself/herself stand tallest in the crowd by doing what it takes to be outstanding and be the one standing on the podium. This is what self-improvement is all about. It is doing whatever it will take to make your-self stand out from everyone by adding that extra touch to yourself that differentiates you from everyone else. How you look is not a problem, the problem is your refusal to make the best of how you look. Your disabilities can be improved on, but are you willing to do what it would take to improve on them? There's always a sacrifice to be paid and the sacrifice is that little extra effort that you're willing to invest in making yourself what you want yourself to be. A boy was called dullard by his classmates because he performed badly in one of their class tests and he was never able to answer any question that he was asked. He got angry at himself for putting himself in such an unpleasant position and decided to do whatever it would take to get himself out of such an unpleasant situation. What did he do? He started devoting more time to his studies. He created a personal study timetable for himself and started paying more attention to his teachers in class. Whatever he had difficulty understanding he would look for someone to explain to him and with time he started catching up. Do you know that some of the people that were calling him Dullard started laughing at him when they discovered that he was devoting more time to his studies? He didn't pay attention to them because he knew why he's doing what he's doing, and what he wants to achieve from it. Sometimes we allow what people would say or how they would react to stop us from taking actions that would make us better and our lives more interesting. This young boy never paid attention to those mocking his sudden seriousness in learning because he truly wants to improve his academic performance. With time he started getting better and having good grades. After a while, he became one of the best students in his class, and some of those that were mocking him previously started coming to him to help them with their academic work. Look, once you know what you want in life and the aspect of your life that you truly want to improve on, you wouldn't allow the fear of what your friends or other people would say to stop you from doing whatever it would take to improve on an aspect of your life that you know needs improvement and can be improved on. Anything you don't have now, you can have, and whatever you can't do very well right now, you can do it excellently well; all you need is to find out what's required to be outstanding in it and ensure that you do it. Your improvement is in your hands. You may not have it now, you may not know it now, you may not be good at it now and you may not look like it now, but if you can find out what you need to do in order for you to have what you desire and you willingly make the decision to invest the time and effort in learning or doing what's required of you, then nothing can stop you from having your desire. It may take time, but with patience, determination, and a consistent effort you will certainly attain it you can improve on yourself, so find out what you need to do to make such improvement happen and do it.

Declare These Words Aloud To Yourself

I am responsible for my growth; I am responsible for my improvement and will do whatever it will take to make myself a better person. I dedicate my life to my constant improvement.

Goals of the Week

MON

TUE

WED

THU

FRI

SAT

SUN

REFLECTION ON ENCOURAGEMENT

....
....
....
....
....
....
....
....
....
....
....
....
....
....
....
....
....
....
....
....
....
....
....
....
....
....
....
....

Daily Journal

MON   TUE   WED   THU   FRI   SAT   SUN   DATE:
○   ○   ○   ○   ○   ○   ○

SLEPT HOURS:

TODAY ENARGY LEVEL:

DONT FORGET:

EXERCISE:

TODAY HIGHLIGHTS

TODAY THOUGHTS

TODAY'S GRATITUDE

HOW TO MAKE TOMMOROW BETTER

NOTES

Daily Journal

MON ○ TUE ○ WED ○ THU ○ FRI ○ SAT ○ SUN ○   DATE:

SLEPT HOURS:

TODAY ENARGY LEVEL:

DONT FORGET:

EXERCISE:

TODAY HIGHLIGHTS

TODAY THOUGHTS

TODAY'S GRATITUDE

HOW TO MAKE TOMMOROW BETTER

NOTES

Daily Journal

MON   TUE   WED   THU   FRI   SAT   SUN

◯   ◯   ◯   ◯   ◯   ◯   ◯   DATE:

SLEPT HOURS:

TODAY ENARGY LEVEL:

DONT FORGET:

EXERCISE:

TODAY HIGHLIGHTS

TODAY THOUGHTS

TODAY'S GRATITUDE

HOW TO MAKE TOMMOROW BETTER

NOTES

Daily Journal

MON TUE WED THU FRI SAT SUN
○   ○   ○   ○   ○   ○   ○   DATE:

SLEPT HOURS:

TODAY ENARGY LEVEL:

DONT FORGET:

EXERCISE:

TODAY HIGHLIGHTS

TODAY THOUGHTS

TODAY'S GRATITUDE

HOW TO MAKE TOMMOROW BETTER

NOTES

Daily Journal

MON TUE WED THU FRI SAT SUN
○   ○   ○   ○   ○   ○   ○   DATE:

SLEPT HOURS:

TODAY ENARGY LEVEL:

DONT FORGET:

EXERCISE:

TODAY HIGHLIGHTS

TODAY THOUGHTS

TODAY'S GRATITUDE

HOW TO MAKE TOMMOROW BETTER

NOTES

Daily Journal

MON   TUE   WED   THU   FRI   SAT   SUN

○   ○   ○   ○   ○   ○   ○   DATE:

SLEPT HOURS:

TODAY ENARGY LEVEL:

DONT FORGET:

EXERCISE:

TODAY HIGHLIGHTS

TODAY THOUGHTS

TODAY'S GRATITUDE

HOW TO MAKE TOMMOROW BETTER

NOTES

Daily Journal

MON ○ TUE ○ WED ○ THU ○ FRI ○ SAT ○ SUN ○ | DATE:

| SLEPT HOURS: |
| TODAY ENARGY LEVEL: |
| DONT FORGET: |
| EXERCISE: |

TODAY HIGHLIGHTS

TODAY THOUGHTS

TODAY'S GRATITUDE

HOW TO MAKE TOMMOROW BETTER

NOTES

Week7

Why You Feel the Way You Do
About Yourself

Week's Wisdom

No man can rise above his/her daily thoughts and words. Your thoughts and words are the media through which you create your reality. Negative thoughts and words will always produce negative actions and results and vice versa.

Affirmation

I make a resolve to think good, speak good and see good in myself daily

Encouragement

What do you think and say to yourself often?
How you feel about yourself is greatly connected to your self-thought and self-talk. I have seen beautiful/handsome teens that are insecure about themselves because of what they think about themselves. I have also seen tall people that think that they are short and short people who think they're too tall. Look, it is not always about how you look or act, but what you think about how you look or behave.

Some people hardly think or say nice things to themselves because they think they aren't all that nice – even when they do nice things. But when they make a little mistake, they judge themselves by such mistake and talk lots of bad stuff about themselves just because of a minor mistake that normally can be overlooked. This occurs because they have already programmed their minds to always dwell on the negative stuff they do and use such a negative mindset to rate themselves. Look, your self-thoughts and self-talk are very important in your life. They influence your feeling about yourself, your confidence in yourself and your actions. If you always think negative thoughts about yourself, it will affect what you'll be saying to yourself often and how you will act.

There are so many people that are not confident enough to attempt anything, even things they can do easily because they have made themselves believe that they suck. You don't suck: you only think you suck that is why things are the way it is around you. Change your thought about yourself and start telling yourself that "I don't suck" and you will start seeing things gradually becoming positive all around you.
Your thoughts and words create your reality. So if you want to create a positive reality around you, you have to change your thought and start speaking in the affirmative.

You may not be actually good at something or not be able to do a particular thing well, but the more you keep telling yourself "I can do it," "I can be good at this," " I can do it better," "I have the ability me to make it happen," etc, you'll start stirring in yourself the desire to want to do that thing and you will start putting in more effort by either practicing more or finding out how you can help yourself to get such thing done.

Your thoughts and your words are very powerful as they both control your feelings, decisions, and actions. Your thoughts influence your words and your words sometimes generate your thoughts. The more you say something, the more you believe it and the more you'll start thinking about it. So by simply dwelling on the positive and declaring positive words into your life daily, you can easily program your mind to dwell on the positive and produce positive results.

Remember, the most important perception you will have in life is the perception you have about yourself. If your self-thoughts and talks are positive, your life will be compelled to produce positive results.

So you owe yourself this responsibility of thinking positive thoughts about yourself and speaking positive words into your life daily irrespective of the circumstances surrounding your life.

Declare These Words Aloud To Yourself

My thoughts will edify me; my words will encourage me, my actions will celebrate me and my feelings will congratulate me. I refuse to entertain negative thoughts and speak negative words about myself.

Goals of the Week

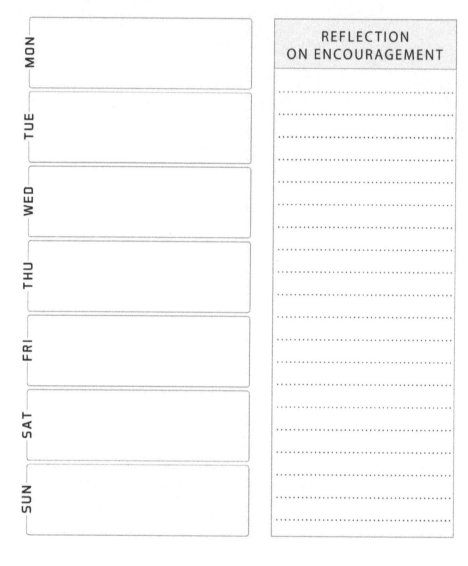

	REFLECTION ON ENCOURAGEMENT
MON	
TUE	
WED	
THU	
FRI	
SAT	
SUN	

Daily Journal

MON   TUE   WED   THU   FRI   SAT   SUN

◯   ◯   ◯   ◯   ◯   ◯   ◯   DATE:

SLEPT HOURS:

TODAY HIGHLIGHTS

TODAY ENARGY LEVEL:

DONT FORGET:

EXERCISE:

TODAY THOUGHTS

TODAY'S GRATITUDE

HOW TO MAKE TOMMOROW BETTER

NOTES

Daily Journal

MON	TUE	WED	THU	FRI	SAT	SUN	DATE:
○	○	○	○	○	○	○	

SLEPT HOURS:

TODAY ENARGY LEVEL:

DONT FORGET:

EXERCISE:

TODAY HIGHLIGHTS

TODAY THOUGHTS

TODAY'S GRATITUDE

HOW TO MAKE TOMMOROW BETTER

NOTES

Daily Journal

MON   TUE   WED   THU   FRI   SAT   SUN
○   ○   ○   ○   ○   ○   ○   DATE:

SLEPT HOURS:

TODAY ENARGY LEVEL:

DONT FORGET:

EXERCISE:

TODAY HIGHLIGHTS

TODAY THOUGHTS

TODAY'S GRATITUDE

HOW TO MAKE TOMMOROW BETTER

NOTES

Daily Journal

MON ○ TUE ○ WED ○ THU ○ FRI ○ SAT ○ SUN ○ DATE:

SLEPT HOURS:

TODAY ENARGY LEVEL:

DONT FORGET:

EXERCISE:

TODAY HIGHLIGHTS

TODAY THOUGHTS

TODAY'S GRATITUDE

HOW TO MAKE TOMMOROW BETTER

NOTES

Daily Journal

MON TUE WED THU FRI SAT SUN
○   ○   ○   ○   ○   ○   ○   DATE:

SLEPT HOURS:

TODAY ENARGY LEVEL:

DONT FORGET:

EXERCISE:

TODAY HIGHLIGHTS

TODAY THOUGHTS

TODAY'S GRATITUDE

HOW TO MAKE TOMMOROW BETTER

NOTES

Daily Journal

MON   TUE   WED   THU   FRI   SAT   SUN
○   ○   ○   ○   ○   ○   ○   DATE:

SLEPT HOURS: TODAY HIGHLIGHTS

TODAY ENARGY LEVEL:

DONT FORGET:

EXERCISE:

TODAY THOUGHTS

....

....

....

....

....

....

TODAY'S GRATITUDE   HOW TO MAKE TOMMOROW BETTER

NOTES

Daily Journal

MON   TUE   WED   THU   FRI   SAT   SUN

○   ○   ○   ○   ○   ○   ○   DATE:

SLEPT HOURS:

TODAY ENARGY LEVEL:

DONT FORGET:

EXERCISE:

TODAY HIGHLIGHTS

TODAY THOUGHTS

TODAY'S GRATITUDE

HOW TO MAKE TOMMOROW BETTER

NOTES

Week8

It's Time To Let Go

Week's Wisdom

Forgiveness is the only force that can free you from the prison of past hurt; while Unforgiveness refreshes the hurt from the past and makes healing impossible.

Affirmation

Today, I choose to forgive everyone that has hurt me or done any form of evil to me in the past. I forgive you and I refuse to harbor you in my heart any longer.

Encouragement

Forgiveness is a very vital part of the self-esteem-building process. Most of us are feeling the way we're feeling about ourselves because of the evil things that some of the people around us have said or done to us in the past.

The sad thing is that some of those people that have hurt us deeply are people very close to us that are supposed to love us, care for us and make us feel good about ourselves. But instead, they said or did things to us that made us hate ourselves or created self-doubt and insecurity in us.

I have seen countless cases of parents abusing their kids, depriving them of love and attention, blaming them for their woes, and treating them like shit that such kids lost every bit of self-worth that he/she might have had. Such kids will grow up having a deep grudge against his/her parents or anyone that contributed to stripping him/her of his/her sense of self-worthiness.

I know a number of adults that resent their parents and don't want to have anything with them because of how their parents made them feel when they were young. I also know of adults that still cringe whenever they remember how they were bullied and wishing they could come in contact with such a bully and pay him/her back in his/her own coin. There are some that still can't believe that they can amount to anything good or accomplish anything worthwhile in life because of what was said or done to them in the past.

Such people are still feeling such a way because they are yet to let go of their unpleasant pasts and offer themselves the opportunity to rise above them. Listen, pal, one of the ways you can keep holding yourself bound by the shackles of your unpleasant past is by refusing to forgive whoever is responsible for such an unpleasant past that you're harboring in your heart. And the longer you hold such grudge, the more you keep reminding yourself of the evil past and reenacting the negative feeling the experience created. You cannot get healed of your past hurt without forgiveness, and if you don't get healed of your past hurt, you cannot rise above the experience that caused such hurt and create a new experience for yourself.

Forgiveness is a necessary part of your healing process and the creation of a new and better you. whoever contributed in whatever way in draining away your sense of self-worthiness should be forgiven; not because he/she deserves such forgiveness, but because that is the only way for you to break yourself free from the hurt of their evil deed and give yourself a new lease of life.

The more you hold onto that grudge, the more you keep yourself bound by it and the more you keep giving your past power over you and keep you from moving forward. So it's in your best interest to let go. You may not have the power to control what was done to you that saps away your self-esteem, but you have the power now to stop such a thing from continuing to sapping your self-esteem. And forgiveness is the only way out.

Declare These Words Aloud To Yourself

I let go every hurt, I let go pain, I let go every

grudge, I set free everyone that has hurt me in the past that I've held in my heart all these years, I lay down every weight of my unpleasant past that I've been carrying aroundall these years and I forgive anyone that has hurt me in any way in the past. I forgive you, not mainly because you deserve it, but because this is the only way I can free myself from the torture of the unpleasant treatment you meted to and move forward. So, I forgive you and I choose not to hold any grudge against you any longer.

Goals of the Week

MON

TUE

WED

THU

FRI

SAT

SUN

REFLECTION ON ENCOURAGEMENT

Daily Journal

MON ○ TUE ○ WED ○ THU ○ FRI ○ SAT ○ SUN ○ | DATE:

SLEPT HOURS:

TODAY ENARGY LEVEL:

DONT FORGET:

EXERCISE:

TODAY HIGHLIGHTS

TODAY THOUGHTS

TODAY'S GRATITUDE

HOW TO MAKE TOMMOROW BETTER

NOTES

Daily Journal

MON TUE WED THU FRI SAT SUN

○   ○   ○   ○   ○   ○   ○   DATE:

SLEPT HOURS:

TODAY ENARGY LEVEL:

DONT FORGET:

EXERCISE:

TODAY HIGHLIGHTS

TODAY THOUGHTS

TODAY'S GRATITUDE

HOW TO MAKE TOMMOROW BETTER

NOTES

Daily Journal

MON   TUE   WED   THU   FRI   SAT   SUN

○   ○   ○   ○   ○   ○   ○   DATE:

SLEPT HOURS:

TODAY ENARGY LEVEL:

DONT FORGET:

EXERCISE:

TODAY HIGHLIGHTS

TODAY THOUGHTS

TODAY'S GRATITUDE

HOW TO MAKE TOMMOROW BETTER

NOTES

Daily Journal

MON   TUE   WED   THU   FRI   SAT   SUN
○   ○   ○   ○   ○   ○   ○   DATE:

SLEPT HOURS:

TODAY ENARGY LEVEL:

DONT FORGET:

EXERCISE:

TODAY HIGHLIGHTS

TODAY THOUGHTS

TODAY'S GRATITUDE

HOW TO MAKE TOMMOROW BETTER

NOTES

Daily Journal

MON   TUE   WED   THU   FRI   SAT   SUN   DATE:
○   ○   ○   ○   ○   ○   ○

SLEPT HOURS:

TODAY ENARGY LEVEL:

DONT FORGET:

EXERCISE:

TODAY HIGHLIGHTS

TODAY THOUGHTS

TODAY'S GRATITUDE

HOW TO MAKE TOMMOROW BETTER

NOTES

Daily Journal

MON TUE WED THU FRI SAT SUN
○   ○   ○   ○   ○   ○   ○   DATE:

SLEPT HOURS:

TODAY ENARGY LEVEL:

DONT FORGET:

EXERCISE:

TODAY HIGHLIGHTS

TODAY THOUGHTS

TODAY'S GRATITUDE

HOW TO MAKE TOMMOROW BETTER

NOTES

Daily Journal

MON   TUE   WED   THU   FRI   SAT   SUN
○   ○   ○   ○   ○   ○   ○   DATE:

SLEPT HOURS:

TODAY ENARGY LEVEL:

DONT FORGET:

EXERCISE:

TODAY HIGHLIGHTS

TODAY THOUGHTS

TODAY'S GRATITUDE

HOW TO MAKE TOMMOROW BETTER

NOTES

Week9

Sound Health And Mind Are A

Product Of Self Care

Week's Wisdom

You can only function or perform at your best

when you're healthy; so always make your

mental and physical wellbeing your number one

daily priority.

Affirmation

I will make my health and well-being my priority; I
will always take good care of myself

Encouragement

Don't ever neglect personal hygiene. Take care of
yourself and don't joke about your health.

Good health is a gift that we're given each day but we
are the ones that determine the preservation of such
gift. How you treat yourself and take care of yourself
greatly influences your health. Watch what you eat, be
cautious of what you do, know when to take time off
from your busy activity, and give yourself some rest.
Don't over bother your mind or yourself with too much
information.

Anything about yourself that you can't change or
improve on, accept it, and never allow it to make you
moody, negative, or influence you to engage yourself in
self-destructive activities.
If you can play your part by taking good care of
yourself and doing all you can to ensure that you have a
sound mind and body, nothing will be able to steal

away your health from you.

You have a great role to play in ensuring that you stay healthy, so ensure that you don't toil with your health because good health is one of the basic requirements for living a great life and you should always make it your priority by taking good care of yourself.

Declare These Words Aloud To Yourself

My health and wellbeing are my responsibility and I will never neglect myself in any way. I will always take care of myself.

Goals of the Week

MON	
TUE	
WED	
THU	
FRI	
SAT	
SUN	

REFLECTION ON ENCOURAGEMENT

....
....
....
....
....
....
....
....
....
....
....
....
....
....
....
....
....
....
....
....
....
....

Daily Journal

MON TUE WED THU FRI SAT SUN
○   ○   ○   ○   ○   ○   ○   DATE:

SLEPT HOURS:

TODAY HIGHLIGHTS

TODAY ENARGY LEVEL:

DONT FORGET:

EXERCISE:

TODAY THOUGHTS

TODAY'S GRATITUDE

HOW TO MAKE TOMMOROW BETTER

NOTES

Daily Journal

MON ○ TUE ○ WED ○ THU ○ FRI ○ SAT ○ SUN ○ | DATE.

SLEPT HOURS:	TODAY HIGHLIGHTS
TODAY ENARGY LEVEL:	
DONT FORGET:	
EXERCISE:	

TODAY THOUGHTS

| TODAY'S GRATITUDE | HOW TO MAKE TOMMOROW BETTER |

NOTES

Daily Journal

MON ○ TUE ○ WED ○ THU ○ FRI ○ SAT ○ SUN ○   DATE:

SLEPT HOURS:

TODAY ENARGY LEVEL:

DONT FORGET:

EXERCISE:

TODAY HIGHLIGHTS

TODAY THOUGHTS

TODAY'S GRATITUDE

HOW TO MAKE TOMMOROW BETTER

NOTES

Daily Journal

MON   TUE   WED   THU   FRI   SAT   SUN

○   ○   ○   ○   ○   ○   ○   DATE:

SLEPT HOURS:

TODAY HIGHLIGHTS

TODAY ENARGY LEVEL:

DONT FORGET:

EXERCISE:

TODAY THOUGHTS

TODAY'S GRATITUDE

HOW TO MAKE TOMMOROW BETTER

NOTES

Daily Journal

MON ○ TUE ○ WED ○ THU ○ FRI ○ SAT ○ SUN ○ DATE:

SLEPT HOURS:

TODAY HIGHLIGHTS

TODAY ENARGY LEVEL:

DONT FORGET:

EXERCISE:

TODAY THOUGHTS

TODAY'S GRATITUDE

HOW TO MAKE TOMMOROW BETTER

NOTES

Daily Journal

MON   TUE   WED   THU   FRI   SAT   SUN   DATE:

○   ○   ○   ○   ○   ○   ○

SLEPT HOURS:

TODAY ENARGY LEVEL:

DONT FORGET:

EXERCISE:

TODAY HIGHLIGHTS

TODAY THOUGHTS

TODAY'S GRATITUDE

HOW TO MAKE TOMMOROW BETTER

NOTES

Daily Journal

MON   TUE   WED   THU   FRI   SAT   SUN

○   ○   ○   ○   ○   ○   ○   DATE:

SLEPT HOURS:

TODAY ENARGY LEVEL:

DONT FORGET:

EXERCISE:

TODAY HIGHLIGHTS

TODAY THOUGHTS

TODAY'S GRATITUDE

HOW TO MAKE TOMMOROW BETTER

NOTES

Week 10

What You're Here For

Week's Wisdom

Purpose creates usefulness and usefulness creates value: thus, making yourself useful wherever you find yourself is the easiest way for you to create value and a positive impression in the lives of those there.

Affirmation

I am a valuable gift to my world

Encouragement

You are here in the world for a purpose. We all have something valuable that we came to the world with for the betterment of our world.

Don't ever look down on yourself or allow anyone to look down on you or put you down. You're very valuable. You're in the world for a purpose; you're here to make the world feel your impact.

Your world starts from your family. Do you think your being in that family is a mistake? I don't think so. Regardless of how you may feel about your family, you're placed there for a purpose. You're a gift to that family and you should never allow the happenings in your family to make you question yourself and feel bad about yourself.

You can be the light that will take that family to the limelight. You can be the star that everyone in that family will see and have a reason to be thankful for. You're are not useless and you're not disadvantaged.

See yourself as a valuable gift to your family, your community, your state, your country and your world, and try to make your impact felt wherever you find your-self in any little way that you can because a gift brings excitement and hope. So be the excitement and hope to those that are privileged to come in contact with you in this life.

Declare These Words Aloud To Yourself

I am a valuable gift to my family, my society, my country and my would; and I will make my impact felt wherever I find myself.

Goals of the Week

MON

TUE

WED

THU

FRI

SAT

SUN

REFLECTION ON ENCOURAGEMENT

Daily Journal

MON   TUE   WED   THU   FRI   SAT   SUN
○   ○   ○   ○   ○   ○   ○   DATE:

SLEPT HOURS:

TODAY ENARGY LEVEL:

DONT FORGET:

EXERCISE:

TODAY HIGHLIGHTS

TODAY THOUGHTS

TODAY'S GRATITUDE

HOW TO MAKE TOMMOROW BETTER

NOTES

Daily Journal

MON   TUE   WED   THU   FRI   SAT   SUN   DATE:
○   ○   ○   ○   ○   ○   ○

SLEPT HOURS:

TODAY ENARGY LEVEL:

DONT FORGET:

EXERCISE:

TODAY HIGHLIGHTS

TODAY THOUGHTS

TODAY'S GRATITUDE

HOW TO MAKE TOMMOROW BETTER

NOTES

Daily Journal

MON   TUE   WED   THU   FRI   SAT   SUN
○   ○   ○   ○   ○   ○   ○   DATE:

SLEPT HOURS:

TODAY ENARGY LEVEL:

DONT FORGET:

EXERCISE:

TODAY HIGHLIGHTS

TODAY THOUGHTS

TODAY'S GRATITUDE

HOW TO MAKE TOMMOROW BETTER

NOTES

Daily Journal

MON   TUE   WED   THU   FRI   SAT   SUN

◯   ◯   ◯   ◯   ◯   ◯   ◯   DATE:

SLEPT HOURS:

TODAY ENARGY LEVEL:

DONT FORGET:

EXERCISE:

TODAY HIGHLIGHTS

TODAY THOUGHTS

TODAY'S GRATITUDE

HOW TO MAKE TOMMOROW BETTER

NOTES

Daily Journal

MON TUE WED THU FRI SAT SUN
○   ○   ○   ○   ○   ○   ○   DATE:

SLEPT HOURS:

TODAY ENARGY LEVEL:

DONT FORGET:

EXERCISE:

TODAY HIGHLIGHTS

TODAY THOUGHTS

TODAY'S GRATITUDE

HOW TO MAKE TOMMOROW BETTER

NOTES

Daily Journal

MON   TUE   WED   THU   FRI   SAT   SUN
○   ○   ○   ○   ○   ○   ○   DATE:

SLEPT HOURS:

TODAY ENARGY LEVEL:

DONT FORGET:

EXERCISE:

TODAY HIGHLIGHTS

TODAY THOUGHTS

TODAY'S GRATITUDE

HOW TO MAKE TOMMOROW BETTER

NOTES

Daily Journal

MON	TUE	WED	THU	FRI	SAT	SUN	DATE:
○	○	○	○	○	○	○	

SLEPT HOURS:

TODAY ENARGY LEVEL:

DONT FORGET:

EXERCISE:

TODAY HIGHLIGHTS

TODAY THOUGHTS

TODAY'S GRATITUDE

HOW TO MAKE TOMMOROW BETTER

NOTES

Week 11

Understand What You Represent

Week's Wisdom

A man's confidence is in his/her understanding of who he/she is and the enormous strength and power at his/her dispousal. When you know who you are, what you stand for, what you represent and the enormous power at your disposal, you would stop thinking lowly of yourself.

Affirmation

I am strong and powerful; I am bold and courageous;
I am tough and resilient; I am fierce and fearless; I
am full of life and blossoming, I am fruitful and
bountiful; I am rich and resourceful and I am black
and beautiful.

Encouragement

Some of us are not proud of who we are because we
think there's something wrong with being black, brown
or whatever name that suits your description of us.
Such people find it difficult to accept who they are
created to be because they have a distorted view of
what their blackness represents.
Some said black symbolizes evil and everything bad,
so they feel bad about themselves for being black.
Some of such people try to hide their blackness by
bleaching their skin, but they forget that being black is
not just about skin color, it is who you are as a
person. It is in your blood and DNA. If you can bleach
your skin in a bid to hide your blackness, can you
also bleach your blood and change your DNA? No. You
are who you are and you are black and you can
never change yourself from being black. So you
have to accept this fact first.

The next point I want to make is, Some of us have a distorted view of what our blackness represents, that's why we are not proud of who we are. Do you know black symbolizes power, strength and authority? Do you also know that black symbolizes resilience, uniqueness and class? Do you know that our presence is very intimidating that is why most people shiver whenever we are around them?

Look, when you don't understand the power you carry and the influence you have, you'll put yourself in a position where anyone can easily trample on you. If despite the serious oppression, deprivation and exploitation we have gone through, we are still standing strong, keeping our heads up and moving ahead, that should give you a clue of how powerful we are - you and me.

We have enough strength, power and influence to make a great change in our society, country and world. That is why they are so scared of us and trying everything they can to hold us down. Have you ever bothered to ask yourself why we are the minority group most feared and oppressed in the US? Have you also wondered why we are the most blackmailed race in the world?

Do you know there was a time when the mainstream media were castigating our color and physique as dirty and unattractive? But do you know that this same physique is what the majority of other races are paying heavily for and risking their lives in order to get an artificial fix through surgery? Do you also know that so many pale skin people are tanning their skin so that they can have it darker?

We have to be proud of what we have naturally. Our skin ages every slowly and can withstand any weather condition. Our skin is thick, glows and reflects our uniqueness. We have to be appreciative of what we have. We have to understand who we are and what we represent. Your blackness symbolizes no evil at all, but good. Our blackness tells the story of our journey and how far we've come. Your blackness is the symbol of your power and influence. Your blackness reflects your authority. That is why people shiver whenever they see you because they know who you are - they know you are powerful.

But it's so sad that so many of us don't yet know who we are. We're using other people's narrative of us to define ourselves. They say black is evil, unattractive, uncultured. etc

and we are buying it because we lack the knowledge of who we truly are.

Look here pal, you are not evil, so don't let any negative portrayal of your blackness make you forget who you are and what you represent. No one else can define you but you yourself. So stop listening to what anyone else has to say about you.

Understand who you are and what you represent. You are a boy/girl of power, strength, resilience, influence and authority. You are an individual of inestimable worth. Know who you are and keep your head up. You're black, no what you represent and be proud of who you are.

Declare These Words Aloud To Yourself

I know who I am; I know who God made me to be
and I know what I re-present. I am a boy/girl of
power; I am a boy/girl of great strength and I am a
boy/girl with great influence, and I must make my life
count in this life.

Goals of the Week

MON	REFLECTION ON ENCOURAGEMENT
TUE	
WED	
THU	
FRI	
SAT	
SUN	

Daily Journal

MON ○ TUE ○ WED ○ THU ○ FRI ○ SAT ○ SUN ○   DATE:

SLEPT HOURS:

TODAY ENARGY LEVEL:

DONT FORGET:

EXERCISE:

TODAY HIGHLIGHTS

TODAY THOUGHTS

TODAY'S GRATITUDE

HOW TO MAKE TOMMOROW BETTER

NOTES

Daily Journal

MON TUE WED THU FRI SAT SUN
○   ○   ○   ○   ○   ○   ○   DATE:

SLEPT HOURS:

TODAY ENARGY LEVEL:

DONT FORGET:

EXERCISE:

TODAY HIGHLIGHTS

TODAY THOUGHTS

TODAY'S GRATITUDE

HOW TO MAKE TOMMOROW BETTER

NOTES

Daily Journal

MON TUE WED THU FRI SAT SUN   DATE:
○   ○   ○   ○   ○   ○   ○

SLEPT HOURS:

TODAY ENARGY LEVEL:

DONT FORGET:

EXERCISE:

TODAY HIGHLIGHTS

TODAY THOUGHTS

TODAY'S GRATITUDE

HOW TO MAKE TOMMOROW BETTER

NOTES

Daily Journal

○   ○   ○   ○   ○   ○   ○   DATE:

SLEPT HOURS:

TODAY ENARGY LEVEL:

DONT FORGET:

EXERCISE:

TODAY HIGHLIGHTS

TODAY THOUGHTS

TODAY'S GRATITUDE

HOW TO MAKE TOMMOROW BETTER

NOTES

Daily Journal

MON   TUE   WED   THU   FRI   SAT   SUN
○   ○   ○   ○   ○   ○   ○   DATE:

SLEPT HOURS:

TODAY HIGHLIGHTS

TODAY ENARGY LEVEL:

DONT FORGET:

EXERCISE:

TODAY THOUGHTS

TODAY'S GRATITUDE

HOW TO MAKE TOMMOROW BETTER

NOTES

Daily Journal

MON   TUE   WED   THU   FRI   SAT   SUN   DATE:
○   ○   ○   ○   ○   ○   ○

SLEPT HOURS:	TODAY HIGHLIGHTS
TODAY ENARGY LEVEL:	
DONT FORGET:	
EXERCISE:	

TODAY THOUGHTS

| TODAY'S GRATITUDE | HOW TO MAKE TOMMOROW BETTER |

NOTES

Daily Journal

MON TUE WED THU FRI SAT SUN
○   ○   ○   ○   ○   ○   ○   DATE:

SLEPT HOURS:

TODAY ENARGY LEVEL:

DONT FORGET:

EXERCISE:

TODAY HIGHLIGHTS

TODAY THOUGHTS

TODAY'S GRATITUDE

HOW TO MAKE TOMMOROW BETTER

NOTES

Week 12

Don t Define Yourself By Them

Week's Wisdom

Mistakes and failures are learning curves on the path of life; don't define yourself by them or make them stop you from reaching your goals/potentials.

Affirmation

I refuse to allow my disabilities, fears, mistakes or failures to define me and stop me from being who I am destined to be.

Encouragement

You cannot go through life without making little mistakes here and there. You cannot go through life without encountering failure. You also cannot go through life without experiencing some sort of fear or uncertainties at some point in your life. But these things happening to you is not as important as your handling of them. Mistakes, failures and fear can either stop/cripple you or you can use them to push yourself to take action and become a better person. It is not what happens to you in life that counts but what you do with what happens to you.

You will go through lots of trying times and painful moments in life, you will make mistakes, the fear of the unknown, what people would say and the fear of failure would overshadow you sometimes, but don't allow them to hold you bound and stop you in life. A courageous man is that man that refused to allow his/her fear to keep him/her in chains and make his/her life static and uninteresting. You are in charge of your life. Nothing can keep you down and stop your growth and advancement in life if you don't give it the power to do that to you.

Don't define your life by your mistakes and failures, don't define your life by your fears and insecurities; it doesn't matter the number of times you fall in life, if you can refuse to remain on the ground and you always pick yourself up, dust yourself and continue your journey, you would certainly get to you expected destination.

Mistakes are learning curves in life, failures are signposts because they show us what doesn't work and point us in the right direction, while fears are motivators. Don't allow them to stop you, but rather, use them to inspire yourself to try harder, put in more effort and do what you can to make yourself better. Nothing can stop you in life if you don't stop yourself. So I urge you to look beyond your mistakes, failures and fears and make a resolve to never stop halfway until you have a grasp of your desires in life.

Declare These Words Aloud To Yourself

I am not my mistakes; I am not defined by my failures and I am bigger than my fears. I will allow nothing to stop me from going after what I love, from expressing myself and from chasing my dreams. I am the driver of my destiny and life.

Goals of the Week

	REFLECTION ON ENCOURAGEMENT
MON	
TUE	
WED	
THU	
FRI	
SAT	
SUN	

Daily Journal

MON	TUE	WED	THU	FRI	SAT	SUN	DATE:
○	○	○	○	○	○	○	

SLEPT HOURS:

TODAY ENARGY LEVEL:

DONT FORGET:

EXERCISE:

TODAY HIGHLIGHTS

TODAY THOUGHTS

TODAY'S GRATITUDE

HOW TO MAKE TOMMOROW BETTER

NOTES

Daily Journal

MON   TUE   WED   THU   FRI   SAT   SUN

○   ○   ○   ○   ○   ○   ○   DATE:

SLEPT HOURS:

TODAY HIGHLIGHTS

TODAY ENARGY LEVEL:

DONT FORGET:

EXERCISE:

TODAY THOUGHTS

TODAY'S GRATITUDE

HOW TO MAKE TOMMOROW BETTER

NOTES

Daily Journal

MON   TUE   WED   THU   FRI   SAT   SUN   DATE:

○   ○   ○   ○   ○   ○   ○

SLEPT HOURS:

TODAY ENARGY LEVEL:

DONT FORGET:

EXERCISE:

TODAY HIGHLIGHTS

TODAY THOUGHTS

TODAY'S GRATITUDE

HOW TO MAKE TOMMOROW BETTER

NOTES

Daily Journal

MON ◯　TUE ◯　WED ◯　THU ◯　FRI ◯　SAT ◯　SUN ◯　DATE:

SLEPT HOURS:

TODAY ENARGY LEVEL:

DONT FORGET:

EXERCISE:

TODAY HIGHLIGHTS

TODAY THOUGHTS

TODAY'S GRATITUDE

HOW TO MAKE TOMMOROW BETTER

NOTES

Daily Journal

MON ○ TUE ○ WED ○ THU ○ FRI ○ SAT ○ SUN ○ DATE:

SLEPT HOURS:

TODAY ENARGY LEVEL:

DONT FORGET:

EXERCISE:

TODAY HIGHLIGHTS

TODAY THOUGHTS

TODAY'S GRATITUDE

HOW TO MAKE TOMMOROW BETTER

NOTES

Daily Journal

MON   TUE   WED   THU   FRI   SAT   SUN
○   ○   ○   ○   ○   ○   ○   DATE:

SLEPT HOURS:

TODAY ENARGY LEVEL:

DONT FORGET:

EXERCISE:

TODAY HIGHLIGHTS

TODAY THOUGHTS

TODAY'S GRATITUDE

HOW TO MAKE TOMMOROW BETTER

NOTES

Daily Journal

MON   TUE   WED   THU   FRI   SAT   SUN
○   ○   ○   ○   ○   ○   ○   DATE:

SLEPT HOURS:

TODAY ENARGY LEVEL:

DONT FORGET:

EXERCISE:

TODAY HIGHLIGHTS

TODAY THOUGHTS

TODAY'S GRATITUDE

HOW TO MAKE TOMMOROW BETTER

NOTES

Chapter Three

Quotes For the Black Women

"It is not our differences that divide us. It is our inability to recognize, accept, and celebrate those differences. " — Audre Lorde

"Love makes your soul crawl out from its hiding place." — Zora Neale Hurston

"Is solace anywhere more comforting than that in the arms of a sister." — Alice Walker

"If I didn't define myself for myself, I would be crunched into other people's fantasies for me and eaten alive." — Audre Lorde

"Don't let anyone rob you of your imagination, your creativity, or your curiosity. It's your place in the world; it's your life. Go on and do all you can with it, and make it the life you want to live. " — Mae Jemison

"Surround yourself with only people who are going to lift you higher." — Oprah Winfrey

"Embrace what makes you unique, even if it makes others uncomfortable. I didn't have to become perfect because I've learned throughout my journey that perfection is the enemy of greatness." — Janelle Monae

"Trust yourself. Think for yourself. Act for yourself. Speak for yourself. Be yourself. Imitation is suicide." – Marva Collins

"A crown, if it hurts us, is not worth wearing." – Pearl Bailey

"Self-esteem means knowing you are the dream." – Oprah Winfrey

"Whatever is bringing you down, get rid of it. Because you'll find that when you're free . . . your true self comes out." — Tina Turner

"You are the designer of your destiny; you are the author of your story." — Lisa Nichols

"Pretty women wonder where my secret lies.

I'm not cute or built to suit a fashion model's size

But when I start to tell them,

They think I'm telling lies.

I say,

It's in the reach of my arms,

The span of my hips,

The stride of my step,

The curl of my lips.

I'm a woman

Phenomenally.

Phenomenal woman,

That's me." — Maya Angelou

"I am not my hair

I am not this skin

I am a soul that lives within" — India Arie

"I'm glad that Shonda Rhimes saw me and said, "Why not?" That's what makes her a visionary. That's what makes her iconic. I think that beauty is subjective. I've heard that statement [less classically beautiful] my entire life. Being a dark-skinned black woman, you heard it from the womb. And "classically not beautiful" is a fancy term for saying ugly. And denouncing you. And erasing you. Now, it worked when I was younger. It no longer works for me now. It's about teaching a culture how to treat you. Because at the end of the day, you define you."
— Viola Davis

"No, I'm not the most beautiful person in the world. Some people think I'm ugly. Some people think I'm okay. You have to love who you are for who you are. I never knock people for their choices but I don't ever want to augment who I am. What I look like and who I am as a gift from my parents and if I want to change that its kind of like slapping them in the face. I always want to be true to who I am because it's my heritage. Even if it's not the most beautiful, it's history and my family history. Beauty is how you make people feel about themselves."

— Whitney White (Naptural85), from an interview with KisforKinky.com

"My complexion had always been an obstacle to overcome and all of a sudden, Oprah was telling me it wasn't. It was perplexing and I wanted to reject it because I had begun to enjoy the seduction of inadequacy. But a flower couldn't help but bloom inside of me. When I saw Alek [Wek] I inadvertently saw a reflection of myself that I could not deny. Now, I had a spring in my step because I felt more seen, more appreciated by the far away gatekeepers of beauty, but around me, the preference for light skin prevailed. To the beholders that I thought mattered, I was still unbeautiful. And my mother again would say to me, "You can't eat beauty. It doesn't feed you." And these words plagued and bothered me; I didn't really understand them until finally, I realized that beauty was not a thing that I could acquire or consume, it was something that I just had to be." — Lupita Nyong'o

"Any woman with kinky textured hair – can wear it, love it and manage it. She only needs the right tools, inspiration and motivation." — Monica Millner

"Who taught you to hate the color of your skin? Who taught you to hate the texture of your hair? Who taught you to hate the shape of your nose and the shape of your lips? Who taught you to hate yourself from the top of your head to the soles of your feet? Who taught you to hate your own kind? Who taught you to hate the race that you belong to so much so that you don't want to be around each other? No... Before you come asking Mr. Muhammad does he teach hate, you should ask yourself who taught you to hate being what God made you." — Malcolm X

"The hair is the richest ornament of women" — Martin Luther King Jr.

"My hair doesn't need to be fixed. Society's narrow-minded view of beauty is what is broken." — NapturallyCurly.com

"Don't remove the kinks from your hair, remove them from your brain." — Marcus Garvey

"Relaxing your hair is like being in prison. You're caged in. Your hair rules you. You didn't go running with Curt today because you don't want to sweat out this straightness. You're always battling to make your hair do what it wasn't meant to do." — Chimamanda Ngozi Adichie, Americanah

"I am a bit of a fundamentalist when it comes to black women's hair. Hair is hair – yet also about larger questions: self-acceptance, insecurity and what the world tells you is beautiful. For many black women, the idea of wearing their hair naturally is unbearable." — Chimamanda Ngozi Adichie

"In particular I want to talk about natural black hair, and how it's not just hair. I mean, I'm interested in hair in sort of a very aesthetic way, just the beauty of hair, but also in a political way: what it says, what it means." — Chimamanda Ngozi Adichie

"The joy I find in having 4C hair is definitely the flexibility. I can pretty much do whatever I want with my hair. I can manipulate it to mimic any texture, or I can braid it, twist it. I can make it into anything I want it to be." — Chloe Lucan, 26 — Silver Spring, MD

"Believe it or not, the joy of my hair is the fact that I have to put work into it. But that's because I can do so many things with it; I can style it in so many ways. It can be voluminous by just getting it wet, or it can be flat by using a blowdryer. My hair can also easily form into a bunch of different shapes, so of course it's going to be a lot of work to take care of — that's why I love it." — Arielle Bines, 23 — Bronx, NY

"In terms of joy, honestly, I'm going to be real: I just look really good. Wearing 4C hair as my crown is how I'm supposed to look. I've had wigs that cost more than my rent, and they still don't look better than what's growing out of my head. You just can't beat it. 4C is good stuff." — Essence Gant, 32 — Augusta, GA

"I find joy in the fact that I can do anything I want with my hair, and I don't really have to worry about the same things I did when it was relaxed. Like, sure, I have to worry about the breakage, things like little fairy knots, and my scalp can be sensitive. But other than that, I do like that I can twist my hair, or I could just 'fro it out, or anything like that. I love the versatility. I've cut it, it's been long, it's been short — it's just fun to work with." — Paigee Keizer, 27 — West Hampton, NJ

"The joy I've found through my hair is finally being able to appreciate my heritage, and understand that beauty is diversified. One day, I'll probably have a daughter who may have hair like mine, and I'll be able to encourage her to love her hair, too." — Danae Reid, 22 — Philadelphia, PA

"People act like Black girls are born with a little tube of relaxer & a note that says, 'My bad.'-God." — Jermaine B

"Dipped in chocolate, bronzed in elegance, enameled with grace, toasted with beauty. My lord, she's a black woman." — Dr. Yosef Ben-Jochannan

"I am dripping melanin, and honey, I am black without apology." — Upile Chisala

"Black excellence, opulence, decadence." — Jay-Z

If you have made it this far, I offer you my most sincere congratulations!

I hope you enjoyed reading this book.

If so, I invite you to leave a positive review on Amazon to support me as a book author.

Thanks for everything and good life

CPSIA information can be obtained
at www.ICGtesting.com
Printed in the USA
BVHW051633100522
636626BV00004B/278